LOVE PRODIGAL

love prodigal

TRACI BRIMHALL

COPPER CANYON PRESS

PORT TOWNSEND, WASHINGTON

Cover art: From J.W. Spoor's *Electro Astronomical Atlas . . .
with Explanatory Notes, Questions and Answers*, 1874.
Courtesy of the Library of Congress.

Copper Canyon Press is in residence at Fort Worden State Park
in Port Townsend, Washington, under the auspices of Centrum.
Centrum is a gathering place for artists and creative thinkers
from around the world, students of all ages and backgrounds,
and audiences seeking extraordinary cultural enrichment.

LIBRARY OF CONGRESS CATALOGING-IN-PUBLICATION DATA
Names: Brimhall, Traci, 1982– author.
Title: Love prodigal / Traci Brimhall.
Description: Port Townsend, Washington : Copper Canyon Press, 2024. |
    Summary: "A collection of poems by Traci Brimhall"— Provided by
    publisher.
Identifiers: LCCN 2024016181 (print) | LCCN 2024016182 (ebook) |
    ISBN 9781556597022 (paperback) | ISBN 9781619323070 (epub)
Subjects: LCGFT: Poetry.
Classification: LCC PS3602.R53177 L68 2024 (print) |
    LCC PS3602.R53177 (ebook) | DDC 811/.6—dc23/eng/20240412
LC record available at https://lccn.loc.gov/2024016181
LC ebook record available at https://lccn.loc.gov/2024016182

9 8 7 6 5 4 3 2 FIRST PRINTING

COPPER CANYON PRESS
Post Office Box 271
Port Townsend, Washington 98368
www.coppercanyonpress.org

for you, courageous enough to love again

You didn't come back from hell with empty hands.
ANDRÉ MALRAUX

Contents

Love Prodigal

If You Want to Fall in Love Again

Meet me in the mint field under a black umbrella.
Half your memories wait there in the shallow burial
of a cigar box labeled *My Once and Future Homecoming.*

The prairie and its empire of grasses aged from green
to champagne, and my pupils are useless in this biblical light.

A stray wandered through the back door I left open.

I gave it your middle name, picked it up by its scruff.
Ticks studded its ribs like proofless rubies. I do that
a lot now, leave doors open. See how little I've changed?

I still cover the eastern windows with masking-tape Xs
in every storm. Once I was in love with leaving, with wearing

a dress with forty-two white buttons down the back.

Now I know that the German for the counterfeit darkness
you see when you close your eyes translates to *own light.*
When I press my eyelids looking for it, red spreads

its knowing stain the way the oil in our fingertips once did,
darkening pages of hand-me-down erotica as we sucked

each other's toes. The months after you left, fantasy

was a form of injury. I catalogued each *what if* in cursive
to try to wish my way across the thin distance between faith
and waiting. Truth is, I put up with your bad waltzing

because it made you close enough to kiss, to push the pin
in your boutonniere into your breastbone. I think I might

be in love again, this time with the finch pilfering purple

coneflower seeds in my garden. You loved, once, the prayer
in me where a prayer shouldn't be, the crisis with a theme.
The way I kneaded breath into the shape of you.

How your absence reefs my skin. How your breath once did.
How you tailored your sentences to almost but not quite reach

the floor. The parts of me that ache for you lately are incus,
malleus, stapes. And when I whisper *Come back* to the scentless
side of the bed you almost do, or your voice does—my heart

in its bone kennel, shaking, convinced it can hear you from
that far, from here, from this home I cannot live in or leave.

Aubade as Fuel

Your lip an abstraction of iris always arousing
the question of the bed. Which goodbye lasts?
Only yesterday my hands rich with dirt. I told you
Milkweed is my new salvation addiction. You know
I always need to save something, to control it.
I can make a pollen island, make your collarbone
a spiritual landscape, the air around us orange
and alive. The shape you left in the sheets
a Rorschach I read as a rattlesnake's skeleton
in the silverware drawer—no, a fire in a cabin,
no, a cabin on fire, the absence it will make.
But look at me now, my heat signature a whole
bouquet of howling, straddling scarves of smoke.

It's okay that it's over. Leaving is a lesson of
pleasure. My ribs, sets of parentheses. My heart,
an aside, an apple ready for the twist. My legs
around your hips, a pillory, our shame public
to the night. Tulip shadows on the nightstand,
an apology marooned and lightless, each bite
mark on your shoulder synonymous with grief.
You ask me to scrape the match against the red
phosphorus of goodbye in a way that makes
you believe it. I ask to be the one on top, the one
struck bright when God pours out the lightning.

Love Prodigal

I make love when I am bored.
That's how I know I'm an intelligent
animal. It's easy to tremble—a pistil
brushed with a bumblebee's fur—
and who doesn't want to be golden,
like pearls of fat glistening in an artery
or a mother's first milk? I want
to send you photos of dead fledglings
on the sidewalk, those perils of the lavish
season, but we are wrong, a news story
tells me so, explaining beauty drives
evolution, not a mate with an advantageous
beak. I wish I could tell you this. Letters
and novels keep seducing me with
their fantasies of closure, but I like
the way your silence wastes inside me.
I am a grieving animal. Let's not pretend
souls are beautiful. They're as ugly
as white petals wilting, crisping
and curling in on themselves
in cloudy water and green rot. But let
them fall into me like loose change
in a leg cast. What's broken cannot be
healed with anything but superglue
and imagination. Still, let it be tended to.
Let it be tender. Let's imagine a miracle
together at a distance, the reunion
of a pronoun and its first verb. I'm not
over it—the elk's blood blackens the bottom
of the fridge, and when I wipe it, it leaves
a pink quarter, blood ghost, hunger stain

in the shape of your birthmark.
I'm a regretful animal. My heart tries
to grow as fast as velvet in May.
It's trying to attract an ending with
a crown of daisies, an archive
of spring, of wants, of waterfalls,
of woods, good God, I know you
won't take me back.

Cold, Crazy, Broken

At the end of it all he accused: *You always had good*
self-preservation instincts. O my selfish survival. I don't
regret it, though I'm sorry I held his breath between
my horns until he explained me to myself, said *cold*
said *crazy* said *broken,* like an owl donating a mouse's
bones to the barn floor, an archaeology of gray.
The end was a table set for twelve, a daisy sharpening
each glass of milk. Before the end, it was like the story
of a woman who woke to her pet constrictor stretched
out against her in bed, tail hooked to toe, split tongue
tasting the salt of her dream, each vein hot with her sleep,
and her veterinarian warned the beloved serpent was
measuring to see if she'd fit. I've woken like that, needed
a doctor to say: *Let it go. You did everything you could.*

At the end, he looked at me, eyes brown and delicate
as a fossil in limestone, and said my love was too weak
to keep him alive. God, I am tired of fetishizing resilience.
I'm ready for a breviary of arrows nocked and aimed
at the blood-dam between rib and rib, tongue lapping
at the garden's gold riot, the sorority of coneflowers
posing for finches suspicious of a synonym that close
to God's heart. I'm ready for a love with hope in it—
plausible, living, holy in its listening, like my pothos
perking when I sing to its vines, or the raven I brush
the wrong way to reveal behind the dark of its feathers
the deeper dark of its hearing. Listen, I become the story
of me—cold as mint, crazy as holding my shadow's hand,
broken as night when the new moon rises through it.

Irreconcilable

Am the midnight
zone, am pelagic and unstudied. Am classical,

the heart's distracted secretary. Was unbaptized
and addicted to sparks.

Am horny for self-awareness,
a slut for emotional work, and am still unsolved.

Was anonymous, even under my nightgown,
even in your hands.

Was nailed tight
like the seam of a velvet couch. Was muddied

with the river's will. Am the bells of too late,
am gaudy and grawlix.

Am organized as an ark
and trying to flood this time. Am not the soprano's

bright injury. Was affection on clearance, glittering
with logos and undisclosed

spite. Am now magenta,
the belly of a cactus pear, the long way home

to avoid your new street. Was a deck of cards
and a magician's false saw.

Am freak, annulled,
interrupted, am the night wind harvesting

coyote calls. Fevered. Blooming. Am not
yours anymore.

The Book of the Dead

There is a name for your skill with small talk,
    and the ultimatum you give before the last one
        is the penultimatum. The sound of leaves

rustling in the wind—there's a name for that.
    Wind, that soul thespian, making psithurism
        in the forest's crown. Do we call honeybees

trying to chaperone the clover the same thing
    we call a romance with chapters missing? Or do we
        admit the way our diaries swelled last year?

I'll bury mine, or at least translate all our sins
    with a thesaurus. What should we name our obituary
        ritual, the one we use to prove we can still say

something kind about each other? Let's try it tonight.
    Let's gentle each other's names in our mouths.
        Abligurition is lost to our lexicons but means

prodigal spending on belly cheer. Dust can keep the clunky
    term—I only want *belly cheer,* a name for glutting
        on lemon pie and vinho verde on days I feel

my natiform heart fasting. What's the word for
    twin solitudes who don't make it to the next
        anniversary? Let's not name it yet, but what can

we call smoke pouring out windows so fast and thick,
    the moon mistakes it for a pond and tries to lie
        down on it? There's no name for the oldest

instrument in the world, no name for the songs
    it played, older than language itself, but there's a name
        for the cave where it was found. Don't ask.

You know I swore this year I would rescue nothing.
    When dictionary editors tried to banish words,
        W.H. Auden put them in poems, evidence they

remained ripe for revival. Unpopular, but useful.
    Still wanted. His whole body of work a love story
        with shifting plotlines and nearly dead language

as the ingenue. Come back to bed, the worst is over.
    Ucalegon, that's what you asked for, the name for
        a neighbor whose house is burning. It's too ugly to save,

but I will watch it with you, the fire with no memory but
    an appetite for the past, ready to take whatever it can lick.
        There is a name for a hunger like that. Like heaven's.

Quiescent

The winner for most patient gestation is
the elephant, and in competition for slowest
force is erosion, wind wearing away the mountain
one gust at a time. Before giant pandas earn
their name, they cub pinkly and mewling, their heft
no greater than an apple. We all need a minute to grow
into who we are. Wait for me. I'll be ready soon.
Croquembouche, baklava, baked Alaska—forbear
each layer, rise, and oven chime so we can have
something delicious, maybe even beautiful.
If beauty's turn is over, let's take our cues from
corpse flowers, which require ten years to bloom.
Instead of strolling by its successful stink months
from now, let's head to the greenhouse to watch
its shy spathe clutch the warming spadix and marvel
at how it meets its own needs for so long. Imagine
what we could make of ourselves in a decade.
The argon-argon clock can measure age by the billions.
Venus makes her fame turn by lazy turn, the slowest
in the solar system, the Saturday morning of
celestial movement. If I must endure transformation,
let it be steady, even gentle. Let's hope I'm a mayfly
with a two-year layaway for wings. Some cicadas need
seventeen. But isn't that a great rest? A perfect time
for emergence? I won't take that long, I promise.
The world's slowest song celebrated its first chord
change in seven years. There were crowds. Jubilation.
Cries that it was worth the wait. Don't leave me. I swear
I am changing with a river's patience, the persistence
of a redwood, the snail's dedication to *almost there*
as it slicks its slow inches up the greenest blades.

Resolution

I don't know why winter summons them back,
    sudden and inevitable as a grand piano
in the arctic sea. And what pulls me back to the pond,

forces my pause, makes me listen to a male blackbird
    screeching vows among the cattails,
his dozen mates each content with a sliver of love?

Frozen trees complain about the wind, unable to rest
    under January's weight, but the birds gurgle and trill,
undaunted by everything's fragile creak. Gravity coerces

a marriage between a broken branch and the water,
    making ice lose custody of a littered champagne flute
bogged with algae and tinsel. Its promise of change sinking

to the milfoil's understory. Its resurrection uncertain.
    A saga for a different year. A group of blackbirds is
called a cloud, a loud fog of hungers. I prefer a cluster

or a grind. A truer name for the unflocking in my chest,
    the nest dripping with smoke. I don't know why the fire
comes every winter to punish me like a mother, to press

the cloud of lonely whistles on the water, but this year,
    I resist. I commit myself to the blackbird. So alive
everywhere. Resilient. The pain of suffering warms into

the pain of healing. Bright and raucous. I call back from
    my shore, yes, I know this abundance. I know—like
the elegy, it will always return, insistent, wild with song.

Refugia

I didn't know I loved Kansas, with its wind skirling
through the arms of windmills, its fields gravid
with lavender, its subscriptions for sunflowers.

I thought I was pollen complaint and water hunger.
I didn't know I loved the hopeful ugliness of cygnets,

or that a group of vultures is called a wake, or that
a skull oxbows with a signature unique as a fingerprint.
I thought I loved to verb through the days, but spring

annulled that marriage, giving me to stillness. I didn't
know I would love the discourse of chickadees

in the redbud and insects at rest on my books, their legs
testing the strength of *n*s and *o*s before flitting off.
I didn't know I would love the sundial's secretarial

shadow. I'd forgotten I loved the blue of afternoon—
bold, bare, the white of ecstasy at its edges, the lyric

bending me over its knees. I'd forgotten how to
recite the rosary long-distance, but I knew I loved
Latin in the shower. I didn't know I loved using

my breath to make a page of the mirror and drawing
vines of vanishing roses with my ring finger. I didn't

know I loved wasps when I set the nest on fire. I only
meant to protect my son from rushing in and out
the door, but I watched them pull pearled eggs

from muddy tunnels, and I knew. I didn't know I loved
raccoons raiding day-old cheeseburgers from trash cans.

I once loved brass bands and free boat rides, but now
I love hammers for hanging pictures and telescopes
for imagining a future with mix tapes of denim and

rhinestone rodeos, my face unmasked, my arm brushing
a stranger's. Even now I love the stout pulses of magicians

and the salads my son makes from the wild in our yard—
the bitter dandelion greens, chickweed, henbit. I'd forgotten
I'm good at survival, too, that I've taught my son the uses

of the earth. Each day we walk one block farther, our own
sympathetic magic, a ritual to ask the world to let us return.

I know I will love tomorrow's moon as it coats its smell
on mint. I'll love the driptorch bathing last year's grasses in fire.
I know hope is a discipline, but so is the dark heat falling

toward me, a citation of grief, a joy ready to welcome a late
continue, to fly open the door for my son, already running.

Museum of Fire

The yard is spangled with a benign pandemic of dandelions,
soft gold waiting to mature into wishes, and we are waiting

for the fevers to pass. We stay indoors, build robots out
of recycling and domino labyrinths, snap plastic Lego bricks

into towers and cars. My son wants to make a skyscraper
that is also a Museum of Fire, floors rising with the heat.

On the first story my son and I make the history of fire,
on the second he wants to make where we are, the slow

smolder of Kansas and its controlled burns, transparent
orange flames tucked into tall grasses. We keep the news

on mute, learn history on toys, and on the third story
we place the O'Leary cow kicking the lantern toward

Chicago. Outside the window, two tulips compete with
the redbud to be pinkest. Spring wants to be a calendar

of bee seductions. Inside, we build the museum's next
story—the Library of Alexandria. My son doesn't ask what

scrolls turned to smoke, so I don't have to say no one knows.
Fragments survive ruin. Dust. Stories. Instead he asks if

the phoenix on the roof with its ersatz blaze is real, and
because I want him to be brave, I say maybe it was once.

Maybe this is an ash year. We must be patient and let it all
happen to us—the consuming, the unfeathering, the body

mentored by pain, a student of its own burning. When my
son goes to the window, he sees it and calls for my camera

to capture it, there in the sky, a myth made cirrus
and stretched but, yes, there, and it opens, it grows, it rises.

A Group of Moths

is called a whisper, all those Xerces flexing
blue apexes on the hush of a poppy's lip until
silence ushers them into a quieter fog. A group

of extinctions is called a grief or that one April,
our Kansas houses coated in dark wings, flutters
rushing down every chimney like sinking smoke.

Farmers say a group of miller moths is an infestation,
but dusted in fallen flour we spread the dead with
tweezers and call them a lesson, an aerial parade

of our missing. Some say a group of moths is called
an eclipse, and a group of eclipses is what I decide
to call a pandemic, suns shuttered like camera lenses.

O all the weeping behind walls before windows open
and the singing begins. But still others say a group
of moths is called a universe, each microscopic scale

the color of an exoplanet or dwarf star gathered into
a flight. A group of universes is called a family fever,
or a drudge of lexicographers might say it is called

a worry, parents rocking to nocturnes of sonorous
moths, cupping a palm over a sleeping child's mouth
to feel the flame of breath gutter but keep burning.

Entomotherapy

More than the velvet ant's queen-of-hearts abdomen
    I love the leaf-cutters, how they eat for two—
        one stomach for them, one for the nursery.

More than the birdwing butterfly with his obvious
    beauty, I love the dull kaleidoscope of tawny emperors.
        More than any other *Hymenopus*, the orchid mantis,

because stillness restores me. Pain woke me again today,
    but already this sanctuary of mind for this unreliable
        body. My son is afraid to hold the roaches

in the insect petting zoo, but more than my fear
    of suddenness, my love of the delicate—softness
        of foreleg and hind, the terrible fragility of wings,

antennae reaching without touching the strange ministry
    of my hand. Today, gentleness is easy. I want
        to be trusted. The pain that rose

through my mother's legs rises through mine,
    the disaster paths taking slow and obscene care
        to crisis each joint. More than a bisected hive,

I want the tube of sweet spit in the gift shop to choir
    on my tongue. I admit it! I love the honey more
        than the bee. More than my frustration

over the museum's lack of signs, my pleasure at factlessness,
    the lovely puzzle of a name—assassin bug, emerald bee,
        black beauty walking stick. I love their otherness,

their manyness, their bodies' vocabulary—spiracle, auricle,
    pollen basket. New parts for function, for feeling.
        So many terms for what hurts and where.

My son holds his arms out and says if he were an insect
    he'd be a flying scorpion. I'll remind him *arachnid*, but not yet,
        because more than truth, my love for his pose,

his imagination, his becoming. More than the venom
    in the scorpion's telson, the stun of its body glowing
        in the black light, how its pedipalps fluoresce

even in fossils. Their whole body detects, teaches them
    when they need to get darker. My son wants to see
        the body that knows how to glow, and I want

to lift him. I want him to pray with even more attention
    than I do. More than the pain reigning in my nerves,
        my love. More than fatigue, more than

weakened hands, a love that heals what it cannot cure.
    And more than my love, the knowledge alive in me,
        testing the light, almost ready to believe it.

A Flower Is Warmer than the Air around It because It Wants the Bee

My fingers grow white with winter, blood
stopping at the palms. My whole body goldens
in summer. Even beneath my bathing suit,

my breasts glow like marigolds. It was wrong
to lick milk off the counter, but my philosophy
is all instinct, and the only god of my hours is

pleasure. My doctor's commandments—do not
run, do not crochet, do not play "Winter Wind"
on the piano. But my joys are sincere and full

of orchids and laps around the track. I want to
abstain from nothing, not the dance parties,
not the red velvet cupcakes, not the prairie

hikes with insects flicking from stem to stem.
I know the curves of my hip sockets from the way
they ache with morning, but when desire comes

with shafts of sunlight and efficient tongues,
I let my body be lightning—so bright the pain lives
somewhere else while I sizzle like a cobra lily.

I have been a spectacle on the kitchen counter
and a cowgirl alone in a cave of winter blankets,
the nerves in my fingers burning white but warming.

Love Is

a patient, perhaps. As in wearing its gown,
gripping its belly and complaining about
its clumsy health, asking for its histories
to be kissed away. Love is kind of excited
to have a body sometimes, with its delicious
weaknesses—shivers, tiredness, the tastebuds
for macchiatos and Oreos. Love is a spring
storm coming to weep its petty joys all over
the bees in the graveyard. Love is a nest
of moonlight, by which I mean nothing
real but still something beautiful, seductive
as any good image. I feel sad about love
as I rub my own feet in the waiting room,
but maybe tomorrow it will come to boast,
its hope will churn through the cumulus noon,
lightning promising a flood of flames, grass
offering obedience to the fire. If it's coming,
I can endure it with the patience of the rose
of Jericho. Even with morning's slow rain
apologizing to the garden, love is a head on
my chest and the deep breath. It's the museum
of confessions and shared sleeps. It is a body's
quick amnesia, the pain barely a memory
after a pill. It glows like a hospital gown dipped
in luminol. It waits like the hand in your hand
for something to stir to life and squeeze.

Doctrine of Signatures

Michael from Adam's eyes the film remov'd,
Which that false fruit that promis'd clearer sight
                                        Paradise Lost

Because the droop of its fruit resembles lungs,
fistfuls of grapes for breath—the asthma wheeze
now sweet. Because ginseng appears human
and ancient, our aches believe in forever. Because,
for centuries, translating pain proved difficult,
and because no other answer announced itself,
great medical minds assumed nature must be a public
and universal manuscript of healing, each hairy root
an analogue for the body and its hurts. Because eyebright
blooms into such an obvious signature, the archangel
Michael gave Adam the mirror of his complaint.
My mother sees the tomato's chambers as a heart's
and scoops seeds with her tongue, her cardiomyopathy
still, still a weep of ticking. Because walnut wrinkles
seem as if they could make me wise, a bowl next to this
year's unjointed taxes. And I'm beginning to believe
my tinnitus can be cured with a mushroom that curls
and folds like pinna, helix, concha. If what needs curing
is the vengeance in me, I prescribe myself bullhorn acacia.
If what needs curing is the shoebox of anniversary cards
in the closet, then the manchineel and its apple, sick
with poisoned milk. And if what needs curing is
my godlessness, the stab of clove in an orange to say
I don't believe in resurrection, but I do believe in
temptation's slow smoke and season, its bright illegal

kiss. If what needs healing is memory, my tattoo shaved off my ribs and gauzed over my eye. If what heals is alive, let me name it, let me bite it, let what is hiding in the tree watch me. Then let it sing.

Why I Stayed

Because the mirror rose over the night garden, melancholy
and bronze. Because I greeted the moon wearing eye shadow

green as a scarab and nothing else. Because like Artemis
I fed a man to his hounds. Because all summer I wanted

to die but chose not to trust my feelings. Instead, I took 99
of the peacock's eyes, half the checking account, and left.

Because I watched spokes of light sow my animus into
a flock of shadows. Because when I catalogued gratitude

I listed high thread counts, gin and tonics, bedrooms with
skylights, jeans on sale and how good my ass looked in them.

Because cabbage white butterflies in the buttercups and
sea-salted caramels never failed to gladden me. Because

I hoped to die painlessly, like a star. Because young sheep
needed their necks tarred to ward off foxes and crows.

Because like Psyche I was careless with candles. Because joy
returned with a kiss crisp as a dried bee that became a stab

of honey on my tongue. Because I wanted to love someone
who wouldn't count my sobs as proof. Because I found

a thousand small pleasures that made me want to live, and
they were bridges, birdsong, strawberries, sunlight, and lambs.

Numb Aubade with Bloodhound

After, I tried to dress suffering up like a plan,
        but I couldn't tell the difference between

        debridement and licking a wound to keep it
open as a confessional. I watched an eclipse

revise itself into moonlight wearing nothing
        but a veil. I didn't expect the ardor maddening

        into grief or how therapy could only scab
a marriage for an afternoon. Not the way my leg

inched away in bed. Not the way I fell through
        a tree like a ghost bird or how a bloodhound

        led me to the wound's evidence in the wild.
At first, I wanted yesterdays folded into tomorrows,

an accordion string of paper dolls, each holding
        the same dedication to kindness. But tomorrow

        foreshadowed thirty-three boxes of books
and the guest-room mattress. The future was culinary,

volcanic, a cherry pie with obsidian crust. It asked me
        to be less of a shape-shifting messiah, and more

        the god a girl needs, more mother than I wanted.
So I let my shame be collaborative and tragic,

like an arsonist dying in a stranger's fire.
        For years, my mirror tried to embarrass me.

        I brushed my teeth, naked and alone. But
the saddest parts of my body were gorgeous,

radiant with vulnerability—apathetic belly,
        knotted upper back, my morning whimper

        and limp before the medication kicked in.
I grew tired of hurting, of time's didactic

gloss revising loss into lessons. I still flossed
        but stopped listing my gratitude for good coffee

        on sale, for the stranger whistling outside
my office, for paying off the credit card.

I even numbed to roadside ditches, those
        oubliettes for litter and hawk feathers, until

        wild sunflowers shook my attention there.
I lost myself. It was a normal mortal

loneliness until the bloodhound bounded
        out of the wilderness—how loyal, how

        unlike me—my heart in his mouth as he shook it.
Joyful, he returned my pain like a gift, and I took it.

Hating the Phoenix Is

hating a myth and hating a myth is hating a swan's wind
under my dress and a wind under my dress is a confession
and a confession is dyeing my hair sangria and hair dyed
sangria is a sadness and sadness is a sane emotion
and a sane emotion is candling an egg and egg candling is
flirting with a god and flirting with a god is a rising and not
the pain it requires and the pain it requires is a valentine
and a valentine is kindling for February and kindling in
February is a playlist of old pop songs and a playlist
of old pop songs is a séance of ghosts and a séance
of ghosts is sexing the shadows and sex in the shadows
is bullying your name to my lips and your name on my lips
is a fire's career in hunger and a fire's career in hunger is
a tax paid in ashes and a tax paid in ashes is a marriage
and a marriage is *Forgive me* and forgiving me is another
weeping and another weeping is a pair of wings beating
red and breathless beneath my dress, alive enough to burn.

The Etymology of Kiss

I've resisted love the way violets resist a perfumer,
refused to give in as easily as roses, run at the first scent
of trouble, peeling off my pillowcase before heading

for the door. But my nose is amorous and guilty.
In some languages, the etymology of kiss is *to smell*,
to get close enough to nuzzle the soft or scratch

of a lover's neck. The hands of the man who taught me
how to check the suspected recluse's back for a violin
smelled like basketballs, but I kissed them. The rest of him

was Dial soap and wet leaves. In the sixteenth century,
women put apples under their armpits before gifting them
to admirers. The lucky recipients could smell that ripe

bodily dew and then taste it, all apocrine and crisp, delicious
at the end of a waltz. Aroma, sweet prelude to appetite,
as important as wind to the sex lives of trees. When I play

the piano, my son sits next to me and counts my mistakes.
The etymology of amateur is *one who loves.* I make him
kiss me and call it a womb tax. He doesn't smell like milk

anymore, but his hair often gives off whiffs of sunlight,
his clothes often pungent with his teacher's perfume.
A man I didn't love back designed a perfume for me

and named it Darkness. He was scentless, lonely. We drank
in basement bars, only made love in candlelight, wore scarves
of scented smoke. Napoléon asked Josephine not to bathe

for two weeks so he could relish her natural aromas. I doctor
myself with baby powder and chemical flowers. I hate the way
Darkness smells—sandalwood, citrus, how easily I can hurt

others because I am bored. When we go camping, I ask
my son whether he knows that even though I don't love his father
anymore, my love for him is infinite. He hides his face

in his sleeping bag and cries. The etymology of infinity
is *incomplete,* so when I say Napoléon planted violets on
Josephine's grave, I mean love should be unfinished.

I mean that when love falls asleep on your arm as you
read to him in your tent, you shouldn't move, you should
listen to rain and sniff his small sap-sticky fingertips, kiss

the forest scent off the knuckles and swear on your new
love for pine, whose language roots down to *punishment*—
you want to stay, to stop resisting what is strong is wild is true.

The End of Girlhood

What else can I say? The book opened
like a future or a grave. I chose a wilder way
through the woods, stalked by a mosquito
whining for my heat. I chose a stranger's mouth
because it rhymed with *love*, because it
finished me off like a sentence. My throat
like a hummingbird's, mistaken for a jewel.
The kiss stuffing my mouth with smoke.
There was a river, a thralling, how I trembled
against my own hand. Of course what I remember
most are the dangers of descent—gypsum flowers
making a forest of the cave, its stones aching
open like hands to receive the gifts—candles,
photos, teacups, my torn hood. The spring
dripped its steady syllables. *Arise, arise.*
I was still myself after, but a new grief opened
inside me like an umbrella. Gentle shield.
Generous shadow. My knowledge made me
soft and unmerciful. All three heads of the dog
turned toward the sound of its name.

Aubade That's Dying to Make It This Time

Burning our first dandelion harvest. That would
be one kind of beginning. As bittersweet

as lemon curd on pancakes or last night's kisses.
The anthology of wildflowers and their antique

shadows stretching the table—a master class
in falling apart before anyone notices. I prefer

to love others—the way giving lets me stay
in control. The bouquet mirrors me and tries

to die like a myth. If I trusted you more, I would
tell you the syrup was a gorgeous waste of another

lightless season—boiled, strained, cooked in sugar,
spring stolen from the bees and mixed with gin.

You cross the river's rocks as I yell *Be careful!*
I love you! The hook of life still thorning my ribs,

scared as a widower's new bride, trying to accept
what's beyond my reach—waterfall, warm wind

in cottonwoods, future pain, the unsteady leaping
as you shout *I accept the risk,* and survive.

Take Two

A museum is the mosasaur's second chance at sunlight.
The tuner is my piano's second chance for my hallelujah

to turn out right. Dermestid beetles are the dead squirrel's
new opportunity, its bones tidy and white in eight days, ready

to articulate the architecture of scamper, leap, and chitter.
The volcano is potentially a chance for opals itching beneath

its surface. My beloved's knees are second chances from two
donors. I chastise his carelessness—the dead shouldn't have to

play basketball. But I thank them sometimes for the generosity
of their bodies. Ghost pipes blooming in August are another

chance for parasites to prove they're beautiful. Not the first,
not the last, but small bells in a short haunting. You could

say chrysalis is a thesis on do-overs, but the butterfly keeps
the caterpillar's nervous system, so no leaf feast or pain

of transformation is lost. And if memory serves, then let it
forget sometimes. Steel made before atomic bombs is less

radioactive, so particle physicists salvage steel from WWII
ships on the seafloor. Imagine becoming a delicate

instrument to detect the unseen after being a machine of war.
I want to be recycled into bewilderment, to die young

enough my lungs can be reused. Schiller kept rotting apples
in his desk, which he'd sniff when he needed the right word.

This sensual leadership of language is the second-to-last chance
for fruit to become a gift. Your body is the second chance

for atoms from dead stars. This is old news but worth singing
annually, a carol full of good tidings. I've always wanted

to have a body I liked, and a list is a second chance at praise.
A bubble, with its sainted hunger for nothing, has no take two.

It is an aesthetic of joy, the delight of not having. I try not to
need forgiveness, but I'm a flawed animal, wild and formal.

I have a serviceable heart full of edits, regrets of conversations
and careless choices. And the doctor is boarding the helicopter

with a red cooler full of iced and packed second chances. And
the head that bows for my confession is quiet, thinking—

my god—love is a career in forgiveness, and boomerang lilacs
come back in autumn to say *Yes, oh yes, we're going to try again.*

Diary of Fires:
A Crown of Prose Sonnets

Even hell is the promise of a second life.
Gold wind converts the prairie grasses to flight.

Listen: I wasn't looking for my own obituary. I'd been searching for a friend's death announcement when I found out I'd died the year before.

Herodotus introduced the phoenix to the West, though he never beheld it with his own eyes. People think he may have confused it with a flamingo or crane, some bird that already had a name.

I heard once that the dawn chorus of birds has no clear reason. Some theorize they sing to announce that they survived another dangerous night with all its unknowns.

The obituary I found was not my own, only someone's with my name, my spelling, nearly my age. I had known she was in the world with her spouse and children, winning races and fitness competitions, but I didn't know she was gone.

In many stories, the phoenix sings before it burns, a sweet song in red couplets. Perhaps it's the same song a lost child sings so she may be found.

I couldn't find my friend's obituary, though I heard he was living under a false name when he died. He used to brag about how quickly he could run from his life—so fast and so far it was a new roommate in a new town who found his body.

Gaston Bachelard writes, *If all that changes slowly may be explained by life, all that changes quickly is explained by fire.* The whole year I didn't know I was dead, I fevered and bloomed wildly, like a tree in a graveyard.

Each time I open my mind to reach the night,
I see cottonwoods licked black by lightning.

When I fear I am falling in love, I fever and bloom wildly, make a
rubric of all my past lovers. I want measurable kisses and common
interests, an objective score for their sexual skills and recycling
habits, the way they season their soups.

In his bestiary, Leonardo da Vinci chose the phoenix to represent
Constancy, *for understanding by nature its renewal it is steadfast to endure
the burning flames.* Accused of inconstancy, the chimney swift—for its
crime of staying in motion, refusing any discomfort.

My new love and I watch documentaries on space, send each other
photos from new telescopes capturing the galaxies glowing brighter.
His mind lives in such gorgeous order; mine survives as a diary of
fires.

Scientists send cottonseeds to the moon, and they bloom and wither
within a lunar day. Sometimes it happens like that—that hungry
optimism before everything fails.

While on their last mission, the crew of the *Columbia* worked in shifts
to perform around eighty experiments in life and material sciences
and fluid physics. As they headed home, the space shuttle broke up,
burned.

My new love teaches me the wisdom of astronomers, who never turn
their telescopes on a full moon, who lights her dry seas too brightly.
The only way to see her well is with shadows.

Shakespeare's "The Phoenix and Turtle" is a poem about the funeral
of two birds in love. Everyone claims no love could have been more
perfect, and it ends as so many funerals do, with a prayer for dead
lovers.

Survival keeps me in the present tense,
utterly abridged. I'm not ready to flee

It ended as many funerals do, with a prayer for my old body. I tried to write an elegy for what I missed about her, before all the waking in pain, the useless hands, the whimpering.

A list of unbelievable animals begins with the fantastically true pink fairy armadillo and concludes with a cloud antelope, fur rich as a myth in daylight. Some days I wonder what unbelievable and painless animal I could be.

But you who live in dreams—Leonardo writes in his Codex on the Flight of Birds—*are better pleased by . . . uncertain things, than by those reasons that are certain and natural.* I don't know whom he's arguing with, but even he drew dragons he knew were lies.

Even the Vegetable Lamb of Tartary grew from someone misunderstanding their own sight—it wasn't woolly sheep but cotton they were petting in a distant land. Who would question the ethics of that imagination, the delight of vine-plucked lambs?

I love my fantasy so much I close my eyes and follow behind it on all fours, still a mammal, still part of the kingdom. Other days, I know fantasies have consequences—God, I want my mind back, my rested, quick, and fogless mind.

In *De anima,* Aristotle considers seeing the most developed sense of the soul. Seeing was the measure of belief, but where does that leave all the invisible truths—gravity, ghost particles, my body's constant emergencies?

In the elegy I try to write for my body, I decide to celebrate my decline: my slower mind, my new carefulness with stairs, doorknobs, deadlines. I make poems a productive dissociation, time away from the body that changed to mirror my mother's.

or question the ethics of my grief—
that gorgeous pain I hold myself against.

I'm afraid to love and become a mirror of my mother, who told me on a heat-drunk walk that if I ever thought badly of her, she would kill herself. So I ran, the word *daughter* around my neck like a collar.

In one of the oldest origin stories of the phoenix, the bird made its resurrection fire from its parent and myrrh. The myrrh that burned was also the phoenix's cradle.

I try to sing my mother's favorite hymns, and my lungs go flat as a catfish skull; my heart knows its own color, the pink so hot it stains my hands like beets. A cosmic mauve perfumes the hellebores—my ribs ache with her voice.

As I cut his hair, my love and I talk about what we would do when one of us dies, and he says, *At first I thought I couldn't live without you—*I pause, take the guard off the razor—*but then I realized I'd be sad for a long time, and then I'd be fine.* I brush bristled hair from his collarbones and cry; I've never felt this safe.

What I most want to understand about the phoenix is its loneliness, how the myth promises renewal, rebirth, but to live forever is to live alone. Fire doesn't even offer the company of a shadow.

Before medical astrology lost its influence, people believed that to become a good physician, you must first be a good astronomer. My mother's blood slinks in me, a hibernating secret, but some people see it and diagnose me as a fire sign.

On TV, recovering the exiled memory of her mother trying to die (*only once?!*) in front of her, Meredith Grey cries—fictional, but grieving better than I do. I think, *Suck it up,* and before the darkness reveals itself, I sear the wound closed.

Smoke forges dusk, ash plagiarizes snow.
Memory sees the truth as a threat.

If I try to sear the wound closed, accept that my body is an image and my mother's is an idea, will the mirror feed me kindness? I know the horror of resurrection is that it's not meant for all of us.

The *Annunciation* was not Leonardo's first great success, though he was the first to take Mary outside to greet the angel. He's praised for showing complex emotions on her face, but how could he know her terrible burning heart?

It takes three to four generations of monarch butterflies to complete the migration from Mexico to Canada and back again. Is the only purpose of all that magnetic memory and transformation to make it home and die?

Stop complaining, it's just a body, I commanded when my mother blushed at the thinness of her hospital gown. Is God untroubled or—when he remembers how he turned away as his son died—is he ashamed?

Leonardo's first great success was a golden sphere mounted on a dome. Perhaps this does not awe anyone now, but did you know the key to this engineering marvel was creating a set of burning mirrors?

The temperature at which a monarch butterfly crawls is 41 degrees, but it can't fly until its muscles heat to 55. Aren't they full of such gorgeous facts, such as how they metabolize what's toxic as a way to protect themselves?

Doctors burned away part of my mother's heart, the most gifted and awful part of her, so when she died, they're whom we blamed. I know I was tired of saving her, but God, if you give her back, I'll cover her shame like a daughter—do you hear me?

O steadfast night, you stunning little liar.
The moon steals the light it borrows.

Something about physics' commitment to flight made me want to cover my shame and say maybe to marriage. If bees weren't drunk on orange blossoms in my hair, then the apple petaling like a tango dress, my flesh lighting the knife.

Pliny the Elder told two origin stories for the phoenix, and it was the more popular version with its easy metaphor that survived—fly, burn, rise from the dead. In the other story, it isn't a bird but a worm that emerges from the puddle of ashes.

When the *Columbia* space shuttle broke open, all the experiments scattered into the sky. A thermos full of *C. elegans*, a species of worm, took heat damage but tumbled to Earth and survived.

An astronaut on the Space Station heard about the *Columbia* breaking apart while he kept orbiting Earth. My love said I misunderstood the astronaut saying the hardest part of grieving was the physical part, but my grief needs gravity too.

One can study only what one has first dreamed about, Bachelard says. *Science is formed rather on a reverie than on an experiment, and it takes a good many experiments to dispel the mists of the dream.*

My love and I try to prove we can grow together, so we claw out last year's weeds, pull free fat white taproots like spines. I fall into the knockout roses, and an old idea of forgiveness begins to weep from my leg.

When my love sees a robin in the yard, I roll pinecones in peanut butter and birdseed, efficient as weekday sex, hang the plagiarized fruit from the redbud, and promise to stay. Heaven help me, this time I do not want to be saved.

I can't outgrow the darkness I protect.
Listen: I sang while I started the fire.

Every spring, we do not save the prairie. Controlled burns cross in thin snakes of fire, and the prairie will come up greener, richer, as long as the wind stays quiet and everyone remembers that fire is a good servant but a bad master.

Many early legends of the phoenix say it lives for five hundred years before gathering spices for its funeral pyre. Pliny the Elder scoffed at Roman doctors who promoted phoenix ashes as a panacea—how many generations would have to live between cures?

I read that Leonardo died feeling like a failure. Researchers traced Leonardo's relatives through twenty-one generations to find those living today so as to discover whether anyone inherited his polymath skills, his gift for self-portraits with red chalk.

My pain is crepuscular, waking itself at dawn and dusk to remind me I inherited my mother's body, though hopefully not her mind. I love mistakes but panic when I think people lie to themselves, so I hold up unwanted mirrors.

Somewhere along the way, people came to believe that phoenix tears could heal too—but what in this world made it cry? I still wonder about another myth; some people believed you could not tell a lie in the presence of a phoenix.

I didn't expect it, the truth of motherhood, the rapture of my son's sleeping face trying to smuggle my soul from my body. To love him to the edge of weeping and know that, even when I couldn't feel it, my mother looked at me with this same agonizing joy.

Metaphors summon one another and are more coordinated than sensations, so much so that a poetic mind is purely and simply a syntax of metaphors,

Bachelard says, speaking of fire and of psychoanalyzing. So, I burned my own obituary—healing promises me a second life full of verbs, heat, and then, and then, the rising.

Arts & Sciences

What if this time I don't begin with a requiem
or a memento mori with a split pomegranate
and a harem of flies? What if instead I tell you

a sleeping octopus changes colors while dreaming,
or how my gender is sable and softens with all
the gorgeous etceteras of age. No one guessed

a chameleon's tongue measured longer than
its body, but it unscrolled beyond tail, beyond
reasonable need. We wanted the mystery

of *Mona Lisa*, but a physician in line at the Louvre
stood staring so long he noticed her thinning hair,
her yellowed eye, and diagnosed her thyroid.

Sometimes it pays to wait. After all, love is
a syllabus of domestic chores with rolling
due dates and extra-credit candlelight. I once

loved someone who hated raspberries. That was
my first mistake. What if this time I love someone
like you who likes fur on a fruit, someone who's

better at suffering, who doesn't confuse their
sensitivity with goodness. What if this time
I think of Darwin, who was sent a rare orchid

with a nectary a foot long and exclaimed,
Good Heavens what insect can suck it. But he knew
that anatomy could not exist unless a moth

evolved a tongue alongside it, some unknown
species with a proboscis long enough to complete
this union. No one believed because no one

had seen it. Victorian women used belladonna
drops to widen their pupils—from the Latin
for *little doll*—and make their gaze a black mirror

so lovers could see themselves. You push me
back to study it, the best distance for beholding.
Always you lament, torn by this choice of look

or touch, but it's time, you say, and close your eyes.
I admit it's easy to spot a forgery with an X-ray—
the brushstrokes too quick, the rendering too clean,

the first draft the final one. Behind a masterpiece—
lavender swapped for gray, a lamb under the unicorn,
a hundred mistakes proving how difficult it is to

become something. You joke I'm the Isaac Newton
of feelings. I can predict failure's orbital speed,
can calculate the chess of silence and confession,

or even the path vines will take to injure the brick.
It's a gift from my last love who made a study
of his wounds, made me balletic, a cat burglar

in a house of eggshells. But what if this time,
I can't see it all coming—not the coup dressed
in Fahrenheit, not you dressed as Aphrodite,

not how I could ever trust your marble hands
cooling the twin crescents of sweat beneath
my breasts, marveling at this wealth of apples.

Admissions Essay

I am a good student. Voted most likely to try
harder. Not voted most likely for fairy tales, though I have
been both hooded and wolfed. My honors thesis on the role
of motherlessness and love hunger brought the candied
house down.

I could've been valedictorian if the metrics
were ardor and potential for transformation. I recognize
the chemical structure of serotonin and how to calculate
my best chance for a free drink from across the room,
and both have strong angles.

I know how it feels when that hormone unlatches
my ribs, silks my legs. I don't confuse that with love,
because in each unit of intimacy, I enter slow. Adjust
my breath. Recognize the accusations that are
confessions.

I excelled in the serious ethics of kissing, how
it makes the body more image than idea, but I admit
that sometimes I like to lick mezcal and grapefruit from
a hero's morally ambiguous mouth. I'm sorry.

That's how I know I'm a successful candidate.
The temptations. The failures. The ever afters of forgiveness
I have already lived. For so long, I offered others the love
I wanted to receive, the cursive letters and lost slippers.
The balanced equations and checkbooks. Years of service
in the scales of care. Change my story. Accept me.

Ode to Oxytocin at a Distance

Let's hear it for the three roses I left on
your kitchen table, vased in the brown neck
of a beer bottle so you would come home
and know. Let's hear it for pictures of my mail,
your gentle inquisition about how to water
my night-blooming cereus, devil's ivy, peace lily.
Let's hear it for dopamine pathways and smiles
when phones chime another cycle of morning.
Let's hear it for covalent bonds, the chemistry
that makes me take a flashlight and mirror to
garden rain to see if I can be like you and bend
the world into ordinary awe. Let's celebrate the sea
between us with its narrative of presence—
my discipleship of light, your patient exposure
of stars. This love is as secular as clouds, as sure
as the atomic bonds of diamonds. Let's celebrate
the cortisol rise as you walk by the lead windows
of first marriages. Let's sing for the short history
of falling, our souls real enough to burn. Let's
do our best. In everything. But tonight especially,
let's find a dark hour to share and glimpse Cassiopeia
straining to dip her glorious hair in the late genesis,
our love working its language over the waves.

Long-Distance Relationship as Alt Text

[A middle-aged woman in an unmade bed posing for her phone's camera. She takes off her compression gloves and tries again, pushing the interdisciplinary erotica of star atlas and physical therapy brochures out of the way. She studies the photo's fortunate failure to translate pain, to reveal only a desire machine, a simpler creature with flexible wrists and hips. In a lifetime of sleeps, they will each spend six years in REM cycles. Her lover says he dreams of her body, whole unconscious years of pleasure he has alone with the thought of her. Miles away, his eyes caress the backs of his eyelids, again, again, ever hungry. The faltering wing of each breath rushes her awake, her body bent as a saint in the burning darkness of the bed.]

I Would Do Anything for Love, but I Won't

cook lobster. They're loyal sea rubies and deserve
better than a pinch of lemon and herbed butter.

But I'll shower hot enough to brighten you, make
zinnias of your shoulders and steal the towels when

it's over, your water-tattooed back a garden before it
fades. I won't shave anything unless I feel like it, but

I'll wax whatever part of your body you request.
I'm not an empath, so I won't cry when I do it. I'll let

your pain be yours. I won't give up coffee or pistachios
or my dog. I know you wouldn't ask, but I like to be

up-front about my boundaries. I bark *mine* like a seagull,
touching my books, my mother's china, my chest,

but you're fine with kindness. You wait for me to feel
safe. I will always let you tease me about talking

to my plants when I water them if you let me tease
the way your hips go stiff when we salsa, but even then

I won't plan another trip to Rome with you. Not this
year, anyway. Not after we've given back the tickets

and calendars, dinners and sunburns we thought were
waiting. Instead let's accept the mail-order lemon trees.

Let's accept repeating puzzles we've already finished,
try the paloma recipe again. Let's accept it's not what

we would do for each other, but what we can do,
and I can feed the sourdough starter we named Gizmo.

You can return my bowl when you've washed it. But
I won't let you say Pluto is not a planet—I miss the solar

system's symmetry. I won't agree that ghosts aren't real,
even if you're right. I like a dose of fear. I like whispering

back to the knocks on the wall. I won't release balloons
when you die, because I love sea turtles almost as much

as you. Maybe it's a tie. I won't kiss anyone after you die
for at least sixty days, and probably longer, but if I meet

someone who smells like you, I might invite them into
the rain and keep my eyes closed. We can disagree about

the shower curtain, can have days without texts. I can
chide you about the state of your tomatoes, and you can

correct the way I say *trilobite,* and the only time I'll run
is across the gymnasium in a pink dress, and the only

time I will give up is in hearts when I count the cards
and know your hand, and no, trust me, this time I can

do it, I can give you everything, even if it means losing,
I will, I want to, let me help you shoot the moon.

Aubade with a Confederacy of Daisies

Love keeps returning with sweet corn from
the farmers market and plastic-wrapped steaks
from the grocery store, keeps lighting the charcoal
and offering me a beer. Love wants to hear about
my day. Love gives me a toothbrush, a confederacy
of daisies, the top half of silk pajamas. And I am
afraid to heal, though kindness opens me like
a pinecone in a fire. Spring's lengthening dusk
remains choirless, though I say *cardinal, chickadee,*
thrush. Night rises, and Love says *Rigel, Aldebaran,*
Sirius, the Winter Hexagon as faithful as Job. Love
waits with the basketball game on and my feet in
its lap, with a newly cut key, with a picture of a glory—
that simple miracle of light—from an airplane window
to add to my cloud collection. Love waits with me
on top, pacified, eyelids soft as an iris beard. Love
waits with an illustrated book of muscles, asks me to
trace tendon to tendon and feel the agonistic biceps
pull against the antagonistic triceps. We are still new
to each other. We don't know how much we will have
to forgive. Love commands quadriceps against
hamstrings, deltoids against latissimi dorsi, and I
slide my finger along obedient contractions. My fear
gentles against the order. My hand tender against
the cords. Pectoralis, trapezius. Love's body falls
and rises like a carousel horse, and it returns to me—
the agony between breaths, falling and yes, finally,
rising, rising, the heaven of it only a darkness away.

Someday I'll Love Traci Brimhall

I'll boast ornament & scandal. I'll blaze & gallop,
       open the burning door with my vowels. I will
make love to myself in a yawn of light on a black
       sand beach & even God will call it good. It will be

as intimate & embarrassing as kissing my wrists
       in public when I want to thank my aching body.
Someday I'll liberate my family tree with a chain saw,
       make a boat of its snarls & paint it red as elegy,

ride it right over the goddamn edge of yesterday.
       I'll crisis & satisfy & let myself cry with someone
watching. I'll learn self-love the way I learned to love olives—
       hesitantly & late in life. I'll be fevered & even

sweet sometimes. I'll obsess the shadows,
       swell with myth. Flawed & propheting, I'll strip
the metaphor to its laces, practice hickeys
       on my arm, bruise myself with the proof of it.

It will be ethical, this love. Its forgiveness will need
       no blood but mine. I'll stop reciting my mother's
autopsy with its anaphora of unknowns. Unbutton
       myself, let the shames scuttle out. Unclench,

heart. Beautiful heart that still has some of my
       mother in it. That nocturnal knocking swathed
in good darkness. Some days I'm spurred &
       baroque, but someday I'll bumble like a bee

through trumpet vines & sympathetic ashes.
      I've tried all of spring's enthusiastic advice &
I'm nearly choosing it. Nearly swinging on ropes
      of moonlight over the wild & darkening fire.

Attachment Theory

Like any good daughter, I blamed the pomegranate,
bled rusty, rosetta, translated the river's darkest reds.

My motive for tomorrow: watch my pansies resist
his frost again, petals golden and blood-blistered.

Mother, it was the whiteflies in the garden. It was
the undisciplined fire endearing itself to the wind after

curfew. Yes, the medicinal erotics of eucalyptus,
the way the polite body confuses the tongue,

my heart as ripe as a corpse flower's skirt. He was
so much hunger and mood, full of wounds you

taught me to heal with silent service. I worried
about his bare scalp in the sun, the mole on his back

blaring pink as a warning. I loved the labors of care,
the aggressive compromise survival requires,

the way his second eyelash yielded half a wish.
I said this time I was loving a healthier version of you

and neglected the roses growing in the lamb's ribs,
snow's patient and ceaseless campaign to hush the lake.

Matrophobia

for A. & G. & B. & J. & J. & J.

My friend says if I'm afraid of becoming my mother,
I should work on my relationships. We've confessed
the darkness of our parents' minds has startled out

of hiding a fire eel insinuating the black ribbon of
its body against the tank's green murk. In a dim bar
in a wet city, we whisper and sip a sparkling rosé,

spooning lamb soup from floral teacups. *Strong connections*
safeguard mental health, she says, so I tell that to a new friend
under fake ivy vines laced with Christmas lights as we eat

chocolate sheet cake, amputated congratulations piped
bright on the frosting. He and I have only met twice
but joke we're lifelong friends, so I can say I am not

my mother. I give him my number, I want more friends
to protect me from the ghost in my genes, and he texts
Every connection is a prayer against loneliness because he'd said

it in person, voice soft as ink, and I didn't want to forget.
My love texts *The blackness of space glows in the microwave.*
Desire leafs in me like burnt paper, warm stain on my fingers.

I write back that I'm coming home and what I want to do
to him when I get there and send it to a friend on accident.
She says she's flattered but knows the message isn't for her.

I feel closer to her because she lets me make mistakes.
The bar walls absorb night like a pupil, and my best friend
says I shouldn't deny people the dignity of their consequences.

But my mother taught me love has a sufferer and a witness.
Another friend says her body is rejecting the cadaver bone
in her finger. I take the hand that's not holding the cabernet.

My thumb on her thumb. A fierce gentleness. I feel the inherited
dark retreating but alert, the black gasping against the love like
the inside of a child's mouth after a mother delivers it.

Annunciation in a Gas Station Bathroom

After I pee and wipe, I creep close, sit on my heels,
wanting to see the electric pinkness, but not wanting

to stroke the baby mouse's nakedness or to grave it.
On the broken door—*The Lord is with you!*

My tongue, ashen and chemical as it was after kissing
a fire-eater, divine word trying to plant itself in the fleshy

nautilus of my ear, but I refuse it. Forgive me. If the baby
were alive, it would disgust me, but my eyes feast on

the gorgeous and dusty stillness. The pleasure of nightmare
is the pleasure of image. The mother mouse is gone,

surviving. So I look. I consent. I take it all in. Sight,
the intimacy that needs distance. Unafraid, I lean closer,

not wanting the fact of the dead pup's color but its
blood-bright knowledge. Glory, glory, it grows in me,

a miracle too new to know the world has a word for it,
the mortal magic overshadowing the womb of my eye.

Prayer against Diagnosis

Lord, loosen your belt of light. Hold your fists as open
as an unread psalm, extinct as kings. I gave myself naked
to your swans, crowned and bloodied, and sank like belief.

Darling Mountain Fire, swear my mother and I are different
enough. Her heart, a babel of magpies. My heart hived
to the white funeral of hours. I grieve quietly, like a parent

after crafting a knife of snow. Oh, now voices, the voices.
My fantasies of faith are not like hers. Dead rabbits
don't cry when vultures discover them. They're dahlias.

Speculative Elegy

My mother died in quicksand conducting
   a choir of taxidermied birds,
or my mother died falling from a tightrope
   after asking if she was revered
or forgiven. Or my mother walked out one day
   with a jeweled clutch of seeds
and pulled psalms from the trees with forceps.
   Or her heart failed. The wreath
of flies she wore to my baptism was always
   a sign. Or her ghost visited—it came
as a floating minotaur and told me to avoid
   narrow spaces. In the rough draft
of my dream, my mother was eaten by a god
   in the shape of a clam. Or my mother
had a seizure and no one could call her back.
   Or her skin grew thin and peeled until
she was sheaves of a blank fable, imagination's
   blackest figment. Or we were wrong.
She never died, so I tried to dig her body free.
   What I pulled from the earth was wet
and red and belted her power ballads to the crows,
   unafraid, as usual, to let her needs be loud.
Or angels unpacked her boxes in the basement
   and traded their wings for her shoulder pads
and blazers. Or the coroner will decide why and how
   when she flew, she flew suddenly forever.

Pastoral without Fairies in the Hawthorn

I am too near to it, even here, even in the headache
of bees in the hedgerows banishing the long dark
of your lungs, the ugly magenta of your afflicted
heart, your body a fever of unlived futures. I think
I could have hurt you back if I loved you enough,
but I kept quiet, already bruised pink as a solstice,
a spell of shrapnel and pollen. Bone roses weep
their liberal praise as I photograph bouquets at
your first funeral. The cheap resilience of hymns.
A heaven emptied of fire alarms. I didn't know
what it felt like to miss someone until years after
you died, and then the pitiless decade pulled loaf
after loaf of rain from me. Happiness is not a cure
but an ending. Clover purples the drought. My hips
wide as a choir of winter butterflies. No one visits
and your ghost wonders why. Why the toadstool
ring stops longing for the changelings, mothers
the empty circumference instead. It is the singing.

What Would I Do if You Returned as a Cardinal?

The light threading through morning's confusion
isn't you. The surprised penny isn't you either.
Hornet at the hummingbird feeder devastates

like wildfires or narrative. Hunger for signs doesn't
bring any. The spiritual equity of the monarch
is still a fortune written for someone else's hope.

Sometimes God is mysterious, and sometimes God
is a knife, an artery rushing to greet the air. Your fear
fostered so much of my suffering. My childhood

a revision of yours. The alpine adolescence—
a cosmetology of fireweed, aster, buttercup. I pruned
your roses, massacre of red flags bloodying the ivy.

God rejected me for my own good. I trespassed into
the matador's closet for the secrets, but I was as alone
as a medium in a haunted house as quiet as what remains

of your body. In the mirror, you and not you. My hair
straighter, thinner. Though I still can't control it, I care
for it. The quilt you never made but the music you did,

your manicure clicking across piano keys. The comfort
of unhealthy patterns blushing harder than rubies.
I would do what I couldn't as a child and turn from you.

Lacrimosa

I like being a mammal, the only animal who
weeps, sadness a foreplay between sodium
and water. I admire my drooping belly for
waxing and waning like a moon, stretching
over my growing son and then gathering
back together like theater curtains. My ring
finger is happy to wear a different weight
these days. Although my marriage splintered
like my parents' did, I believe vows can make
some people open like a peony, a hundred
vulnerable layers lying against one another.

I want to rejoice that I'm finally learning how
to French braid my own hair, but it is strange
to be an animal who can remember bubblegum
sunsets, clotheslines pinned with drying flowers,
winter's generosity of stars. All that beauty
staining my pupils makes me weep, which
makes me remember someone studied
the fractals of tears under a microscope,
so much stunning geometry spilling from me
at each onion and stubbed toe and heartbreak.
My tears' chemistry—a marvel, a miracle even.

I used to want my heart to be an ocean, not
this river heart eddying in the slightest pain
but a gorgeous boss of an organ that could
contain everything, even secrets. In another life,
I might have married someone with a fishpond
heart like my father's, so reliable in its seasons.

In this life I married my mother's Mariana Trench
heart with its pressure, its deforming gravity.

I went nearly a decade without crying, but once
I understood my heart would always need me
to swaddle it in music and promise to be kind,
it let me weep again, whole wet pillowcases
full of grief. I bought a lachrymatory to catch
all my splendid tears and save them, because
I like that I am a messy animal full of melancholy
with working knees and toes that crack when
I walk downstairs, weak hands and a softening
chin that makes me see my mother in the mirror,
crying her famous tears, this time saying
she loves what I've done with my hair.

Joy: A Reprise

When I first learned the divorce rate
among barn owls, I felt a thrill not unlike
the sight of my beloved, panting after

a bike ride, Rorschaching my kitchen floor
with sweat, each wet blister blooming
hormone and oak. Wonder is like that,

always using knowledge as foreplay.
The strongest muscle in the human body
is the tongue, and I keep mine in training,

heroic, ready for Olympic kisses. Joy is
a gold cantata—no, sonata—no, the wild timbre
of my name in his mouth. When the pair

separates, it's the male barn owl who tends
to keep the house. It's alright, though. Who
needs sticks and rafters and fights over who

heard the last mouse beneath snow? I have
a good imagination, but in every constellation,
I see triangle upon triangle, the terror of repetition,

unbroken cycle of wounds in need of saviors.
My beloved insists not everything is a pattern.
But still, I hear echoes and try to see the night

sky as lions, as fish, as a light garden, as a goddess
wetting her hair in darkness's possibility.
I like knowing that a barn owl's second mate

tends to stick. Compatibility takes some
practice. A good statistic can be a consolation.
Ecstasy bites deep, but joy's furrows heal

under flannel pajamas. My heart built its bluest
iterations on the smallest and most possible
pleasures—shared crème brûlée, a puzzle

of lunar seas, scavenger hunts, the ruthless
surprise of daisies spilling from the lap of
a second chance in a bed of sunflowers.

Love Languages

You rank them from the flamboyance of cactus
blossoms to the ponderosa altitude. I order mine
with acts of solitude at the top, my thumb

in the soft rough of a daisy's eye at the bottom.
Best of all we understand each other's metaphors,
how the architectures we make with our hands—

geometry of cathedrals, nautilus of a fist—
are an evolving lexicon for what grows or deepens
or opens a door to an anthology of rings, but no matter

our synonyms for *My god, there's more of this,*
we watch our verbs, the connotations they muster
after the noun. Other loves used body parts for

our names, but we're careful with our arguments,
make adjectives a generous holding, a patient copyedit.
My love language is phonetic, spelling itself in batches

of home brew, in our bedroom window's archive of light,
the gentle ministry of basil sprouts. Our love is an imperative
sentence, or a sentencing, but both make silence feel

dangerous, so I write *Maybe forever?* on your back
in cursive. The answer comes home before the storm
when, the front door gaping, you pull me from the couch,

sprint up the hot sidewalk to the top of this hill
to show me an anvil cloud you call the most amazing
you've ever seen as you look at me, waiting for

my astonishment at how you say it can all change—
wordless, sudden as a hummingbird—and be thunderous
and aching and rapturous and so terribly, terribly bright.

I Want to Write an Epithalamium for Our Future

I do, I want to say it, but for years I made a labor
of my sadness, a professional sorrow. But you,

you're bold as a New York pigeon, a joy with stamina.
Your body, my midnight bull's-eye, a secret unfit for

these blushing lines. And the future is unspoken
and full of transplanted irises, each needing a year

of rest before they bloom again. The shock of it,
the forgetting, and then the soft purple blades rising

to bruise the beds. I want to trust again, but my friend
is a burning mirror. He can say it now—*love*—but he also

sleeps with cyanide under his pillow. He says it's a joke,
but he also says he can't survive another divorce.

Our hope is the eel's pharyngeal jaws, which is to say
doubled and tenacious. I took my time falling in love

with what I am. You once celebrated my no, so I give
you my curious yes, my *what if*s no longer corseted

in anxiety but as sure as Leonardo gluing raw silk to pine,
his wings only waiting for the right wind. The home

we make in each other is quiet enough I hear ghosts
still troubling the attic. My friend is made of loon stories,

not all of which I should know, but he did tell me about
the eagle lifted from the lake, a clean hole where its heart

should be, which means I could have kissed other mouths
in other gardens, trembling like wisteria. I could still ask

my friend for the exit, let bitter almond season my sheets.
Instead, my hand in yours, choosing your well-worn drum,

your acrobatic heart steady in its holding, astounding
in its aerial feats. The happiness finally possible.

Aubade on a Ghost Hunt

We prefer to do it with the lights on,
the Victrola scratching *How long can it last?*
against the tremble of curtains. Patient,
we learn the walls, their glossary of knocks,
translating harlequin and dust. What we
know lives here—lonely bone-star blossom
of the spider plant, lost bee on the sill,
tape recorder's static alive and puckering.
I tell you our future is the guttering candle
in the basement birdcage. *Prove it*, you say,
and I set both its shadows swaying. Our history,
the attic window, how the unseen surprises
the photograph. You ask what there is
to be afraid of. I ask the past to make itself
known to me. We only have to make it through
the night, so we close the dolls' eyes. Danger
midwifes the heart's spring. We are cabbage roses
grooming the parlor air with unsexed pistils.
I have this kiss and its sleepless itinerary.
Your lip, pink logic and cushion. The door
tests its lock, and I let you ruin each light
orb and whisper with physics. If we're sure
something is here, then we have to find out
what it wants. A voice on the recorder, sweet
as gravecakes—*Don't go.* We can admit it wasn't
proof we came for, it was the question.

Body, Remember

Wake up, nerves. Remember touch, breath, touch.
O body, remember those mouths, those hands,
how you desired all of it, especially blindfolded.

The best of everything has been love, those pounds
of joy. Forget toes stubbed on bed edges, bike pedals
hitting shins, joints sugar-swollen and complaining.

Remember the fetal Doppler looping lemniscates
over your torso, listening for the baby but finding
the native darkness of your interior, blood rushing

like horses galloping underwater? And remember
those pop songs you danced to in darkened kitchens
so passing cars couldn't see your hips' enthusiasm

for a good bass line? Remember last night—the car's
engine bragging its speed, shaking the marrow of each
bone? You were alive with a great rage, monstrous

and capable. But don't worry, you were only an animal.
One day you'll get to die like everything you admire,
and your beloved will forget your face. Remember

it is not because he failed to love you well, but because
his brain doesn't hold faces. Your brain will hold so
little then, too, so you can become what's next. It will

be beautiful, body, your cells undressing, forgetting.
And over legs you endlessly shaved, grasses will grow
like you—eager, wild, surviving every day they can.

Will & Testament

Before I let go, let me be awake for midnight again, the new moon
and I both comfortable in our tenure with darkness. Before it's over,
I want to testify about your untrustworthy mouth, how it rushes off
my breasts too fast, my pleasure under threat. If I get to choose

an afterlife, I'd pick the one with never-ending snow for what it does
to the silence, how it makes it easier to hear God listening. Before
these years with you, my words were pregnant with an ugly sadness.
Now I want a house of nights, of dialogues with owls, of homemade

peanut-butter ice cream and your ankle on mine. Now that there's
this fire, the river. Now that my body warned us of its limits, the plan.
Now with this love, I want to answer the valentine ringing in the bottle.
I want to drop the clock from a hot-air balloon before my body ends

up in a cadaver lab or a carnival ride. We celebrate my birthday by
moving our rings to our right hands to make a happier future possible.
I ask how long you will wait after I die to move on. You promise to
entomb me like a pharaoh—with a chariot and fifty pairs of underwear.

Resurrection has practical concerns. Bury me with one of your shirts
in case I come back as a bloodhound. Save my favorite panties—
the pink ones—for a sexier immortality or a lonely evening. I would
return to you as any star. Stay awake. Be ready. I'm already burning.

Notes

"Irreconcilable" is after Lucie Brock-Broido's "Am Moor."

"Refugia" is after Nâzim Hikmet's "Things I Didn't Know I Loved."

"Hating the Phoenix Is" is after Jenny Molberg's "Loving Ophelia Is."

"The Etymology of Kiss" owes a great debt to Diane Ackerman's *A Natural History of the Senses* for all those wonderful facts about smells.

"Diary of Fires: A Crown of Prose Sonnets" references the following works: Gaston Bachelard's *The Psychoanalysis of Fire*; Joseph Nigg's *The Phoenix: An Unnatural Biography of a Mythical Beast*; and Francesca Fiorani's *The Shadow Drawing: How Science Taught Leonardo How to Paint*. It also references *Grey's Anatomy*, Aristotle's *De anima*, and astronaut Ken Bowersox in *When We Left Earth: The NASA Missions*.

"Someday I'll Love Traci Brimhall" is after Ocean Vuong's "Someday I'll Love Ocean Vuong," which is after Roger Reeves's "Someday I'll Love Roger Reeves" and Frank O'Hara's "Katy."

"Body, Remember" is after C.P. Cavafy's "Remember, Body."

"Will & Testament" began as a response to Alex Dimitrov's "Poem for the Reader" in his book *Love and Other Poems*.

The aubades were written in response to poems in my first book, *Rookery*. Resurrecting my love for poetry meant going back to the beginning to wait with a golf club in a lightning storm and see whether I could bring the fire back to me.

Acknowledgments

The Adroit Journal: "Cold, Crazy, Broken" and "Prayer against Diagnosis"

The American Poetry Review: "If You Want to Fall in Love Again," "I Want to Write an Epithalamium for Our Future," and "I Would Do Anything for Love, but I Won't"

The Believer: "Annunciation in a Gas Station Bathroom"

Copper Nickel: "A Group of Moths"

EcoTheo Review: "The End of Girlhood"

Green Mountains Review: "The Etymology of Kiss" and "Love Languages"

Iron Horse Literary Review: "Matrophobia"

The Kenyon Review: "Pastoral without Fairies in the Hawthorn"

Michigan Quarterly Review: "Long-Distance Relationship as Alt Text"

Narrative: "The Book of the Dead," "Joy: A Reprise," and "Quiescent"

The Nation: "Love Prodigal"

NELLE: "Speculative Elegy"

The New Yorker: "Arts & Sciences" and "Aubade as Fuel"

Nimrod: "Entomotherapy" and "Lacrimosa"

One: "Someday I'll Love Traci Brimhall"

Ploughshares: "Irreconcilable"

Plume: "A Flower Is Warmer than the Air around It because It Wants the Bee" and "Love Is"

Poetry Ireland Review: "Why I Stayed"

Quarterly West: "Will & Testament"

Southeast Review: "Aubade with a Confederacy of Daisies" and "Ode to Oxytocin at a Distance"

Southern Indiana Review: "Attachment Theory," "Aubade That's Dying to Make It This Time," and "Numb Aubade with Bloodhound"

SWWIM Every Day: "Admissions Essay"

Terrain.org: "Refugia"

32 Poems: "Hating the Phoenix Is"

"Aubade on a Ghost Hunt" appeared in the Poem-a-Day series from the Academy of American Poets. (Thanks, Safiya Sinclair!)

"Doctrine of Signatures" received the Cecil Hemley Memorial Award from the Poetry Society of America, selected by Sally Wen Mao.

"Resolution" appeared in *Words of a Feather,* edited by Megan Kaminski.

Gratitude

More than half this book was written with Brynn Saito on our summer travels. Loving her, and enjoying her friendship, is one of the great gifts of my life.

My Monday night poetry group also keeps me making work and talking about poems, and while the group changes (and I don't want to forget anyone), thank you: Brennan Bestwick, Jacque Boucher, Maia Carlson, Luisa Muradyan, Ania Payne, and Eileen Wertzberger.

Other friends have also asked for poetry exchanges and brought me real talk and line breaks. My gratitude for the fantastic Katy Martin, Charlotte Pence, and Martin Rock.

Thank you also to the residencies that offered me space and time to write some of these poems: Kimmel Harding Nelson Center for the Arts, Moth Retreat, the National Park Service Artist-in-Residence program, SWWIM/The Betsy Writer's Room, and The Writers' Colony at Dairy Hollow.

And my immense gratitude to the staff at Copper Canyon: Janeen Armstrong, Joseph Bednarik, Claretta Holsey, Julie Johnson, Bruce Kelley, George Knotek, Jessica Roeder, Kaci X. Tavares, Marisa Vito, Michael Wiegers, and Ryo Yamaguchi. And to the extraordinary Ashley E. Wynter, thank you so very much for helping me find and refine this diary of fires.

About the Author

Traci Brimhall is the author of *Love Prodigal* (2024); *Come the Slumberless to the Land of Nod* (2020); *Saudade* (2017); *Our Lady of the Ruins* (2012), selected by Carolyn Forché for the Barnard Women Poets Prize; and *Rookery* (2010), selected by Michelle Boisseau for the Crab Orchard Series in Poetry First Book Award and finalist for the Foreword Book of the Year Award. Her work has received a Pushcart Prize, and she has been honored as a Laureate Fellow for the Academy of American Poets, an Artist-in-Residence for the National Parks Service, and a Literature Fellow in Poetry for the National Endowment for the Arts. She holds degrees from Florida State University (BA), Sarah Lawrence College (MFA), and Western Michigan University (PhD). She is currently a professor of English at Kansas State University and the poet laureate of Kansas.

Poetry is vital to language and living. Since 1972, Copper Canyon Press has published extraordinary poetry from around the world to engage the imaginations and intellects of readers, writers, booksellers, librarians, teachers, students, and donors.

WE ARE GRATEFUL FOR THE MAJOR SUPPORT PROVIDED BY:

academy of american poets

OFFICE OF ARTS & CULTURE
SEATTLE

ARTSFUND

THE PAUL G. ALLEN FAMILY FOUNDATION

Hawthornden Foundation

POETRY FOUNDATION

INGRAM CONTENT GROUP

the point
envision·enact·evolve

MCSWEENEY'S

WASHINGTON STATE ARTS COMMISSION

ART WORKS.
National Endowment for the Arts
arts.gov

The Witter Bynner Foundation for Poetry

TO LEARN MORE ABOUT UNDERWRITING
COPPER CANYON PRESS TITLES,
PLEASE CALL 360-385-4925 EXT. 105

WE ARE GRATEFUL FOR THE MAJOR SUPPORT PROVIDED BY:

Anonymous

Jill Baker and Jeffrey Bishop

Anne and Geoffrey Barker

Donna Bellew

Will Blythe

John Branch

Diana Broze

John R. Cahill

Sarah J. Cavanaugh

Keith Cowan and Linda Walsh

Peter Currie

The Evans Family

Mimi Gardner Gates

Gull Industries Inc.
   on behalf of William True

Carolyn and Robert Hedin

David and Jane Hibbard

Bruce S. Kahn

Phil Kovacevich and Eric Wechsler

Maureen Lee and Mark Busto

Ellie Mathews and Carl Youngmann
   as The North Press

Larry Mawby and Lois Bahle

Petunia Charitable Fund and
   adviser Elizabeth Hebert

Suzanne Rapp and Mark Hamilton

Adam and Lynn Rauch

Emily and Dan Raymond

Joseph C. Roberts

Cynthia Sears

Kim and Jeff Seely

Tree Swenson

Julia Sze

Barbara and Charles Wright

In honor of C.D. Wright
   from Forrest Gander

Caleb Young as C. Young Creative

The dedicated interns and faithful
   volunteers of Copper Canyon Press

The pressmark for Copper Canyon Press
suggests entrance, connection, and interaction
while holding at its center
an attentive, dynamic space for poetry.

This book is set in Verdigris MVB Pro Text.
Book design by Gopa & Ted2, Inc.
Printed on archival-quality paper.